A GUATEMALAN FAMILY

A GUATEMALAN FAMILY

By Michael Malone

Lerner Publications Company • Minneapolis

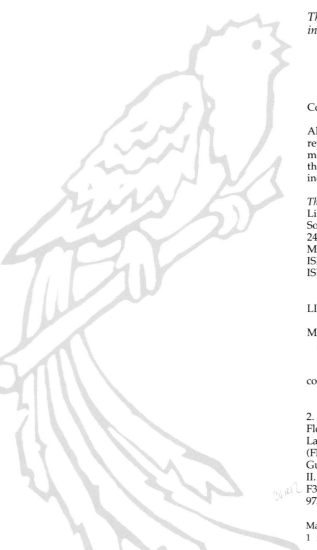

The interviews for this book were conducted in the fall of 1994 and in 1995.

This book is available in two editions:
Library binding by Lerner Publications Company
Soft cover by First Avenue Editions
241 First Avenue North
Minneapolis, MN 55401
ISBN: 0–8225–3400–2 (lib. bdg.)
ISBN: 0–8225–9742–X (pbk.)

LIBRARY OF CONGRESS CATALOGING-IN-PUBLICATION DATA

Malone, Michael.
    A Guatemalan family / by Michael Malone.
        p.   cm. — (Journey between two worlds)
        Summary: Describes a Guatemalan family's struggle to emigrate from their country to the United States and the adjustments they have made.
        ISBN 0–8225–3400–2 (lib. bdg.)
        1. Guatemalan American families—Florida—Lake Worth—Juvenile literature. 2. Refugees, Political—Guatemala—Juvenile literature. 3. Refugees, Political—Florida—Lake Worth—Juvenile literature. 4. Guatemalan Americans—Florida—Lake Worth—Social life and customs—Juvenile literature. 5. Lake Worth (Fla.)—Social life and customs—Juvenile literature. 6. Human rights—Guatemala—Juvenile literature. [1. Guatemalan Americans. 2. Refugees] I. Title. II. Series.
    F319.L196M35 1996
    975.9'32—dc20   95–33521

Manufactured in the United States of America
1 2 3 4 5 6 – JR – 01 00 99 98 97 96

AUTHOR'S NOTE

I am indebted to the Guatemalan community and their friends in South Florida who generously shared their experience and knowledge. A special thanks to Don José and Maria Mendez, who trusted a stranger with their courageous story. To Karin and her brothers, may the sacredness of your past guide you always.

To my wife and soulmate, Chris, and daughters, Raen and Kayla, many many thanks.

War and poverty have forced many people in the Central American nation of Guatemala to leave their country.

SERIES INTRODUCTION

 What they have left behind is sometimes a living nightmare of war and hunger that most Americans can hardly begin to imagine. As refugees set out to start a new life in another country, they are torn by many feelings. They may wish they didn't have to leave their homeland. They may fear giving up the only life they have ever known. Many may also feel excitement and hope as they struggle to build a better life in a new country.

People who move from one place to another are called migrants. Two types of migrants are immigrants and refugees. Immigrants choose to leave their homelands, usually to improve their standards of living. They may be leaving behind poverty, famine (hunger), or a failing economy. They may be pursuing a better job or reuniting with family members.

Guatemalans buy food and other goods at street markets.

Refugees, on the other hand, often have no choice but to flee their homeland to protect their own personal safety. How could anyone be in so much danger? The government of his or her country is either unable or unwilling to protect its citizens from persecution, or cruel treatment. In many cases, the government is actually the cause of the persecution. Government leaders or another group within the country may be persecuting anyone of a certain race, religion, or ethnic background. Or they may persecute those who belong to a particular social group or who hold political opinions that are not accepted by the government.

From the 1950s through the mid-1970s, the number of refugees worldwide held steady at between 1.5 and 2.5 million. The number began to rise sharply in 1976. By the mid-1990s, it approached 20 million. These figures do not include people who are fleeing disasters such as famine (estimated to be at least 10 million). Nor do they include those who are forced to leave their homes but stay within their own countries (about 27 million).

As this rise in refugees and other migrants continues, countries that have long welcomed newcomers are beginning to close their doors. Some U.S. citizens question whether the United States should accept refugees when it cannot even meet the needs of all its own people. On the other hand, experts point out that the number of refugees is small—less than 20 percent of all migrants worldwide—so refugees really don't have a very big impact on the nation. Still others suggest that the tide of refugees could be slowed through greater efforts to address the problems that force people to flee. There are no easy answers in this ongoing debate.

This book is one in a series called *Journey Between Two Worlds*, which looks at the lives of refugee families—their difficulties and triumphs. Each book describes the journey of a family from their homeland to the United States and how they adjust to a new life in America while still preserving traditions from their homeland. The series makes no attempt to join the debate about refugees. Instead, *Journey Between Two Worlds* hopes to give readers a better understanding of the daily struggles and joys of a refugee family.

Carrying their belongings on their backs, Guatemalans wade through a stream (top) *to get to a refugee camp in neighboring Mexico. Some refugees hide in trucks* (right) *or other vehicles to leave Guatemala.*

Ya me voy, ya me voy
Porque no soy de aquí.
Soy de un pueblo muy lejano,
Yo soy de San Miguel Acatán.

I'm going away, I'm going away
Because I'm not from here.
I'm from a town far away
I'm from San Miguel Acatán.

(Song played on the marimba and sung at celebrations in San Miguel Acatán, Guatemala).

 "Come out Chepe Mendez! If you don't surrender, we will kill you." The shouting outside her bedroom window startled Maria Mendez. The noise and rat-tat-tat of machine gun fire began at the far end of San Miguel Acatán, the Guatemalan village where Maria lived. Then, gun burst by gun burst, the chaos edged closer. Maria froze in her bed.

Once quiet and peaceful, life in Guatemala's villages has been disrupted by war.

The guerillas believed that Don José was a government sympathizer like these members of a government-formed militia.

Now the *guerrillas* (peasant soldiers) pounded on the front door and called for her father-in-law, José Mendez. Those who knew him well called him "Chepe," a Spanish nickname for José. Maria slid from her grass-stuffed mattress and tiptoed across the cool dirt floor. Her baby, Josito (little José), whimpered in his crib. Maria cradled him in her strong brown arms. *"Cállate, querido* (quiet, dear one)," she whispered. His mother's warmth and familiar scent quieted Josito.

Maria slipped the infant into the baby sling on her back and crept toward the window. Peering into the dusty, starlit street, she saw the guerrillas for the first time. Masks covered their faces, and the peasant soldiers paced back and forth, clutching their rifles anxiously. The shadows of their guns on the mud-brick walls were huge and terrifying.

"Why had these masked soldiers come to San Miguel Acatán?" Maria wondered. "What did they want with Don José?" (*Don* is a Spanish title similar to "sir," used to show respect.)

For years, Maria had heard rumors about the "hidden war." A ragtag army of angry citizens, mostly poor people, had banded together to fight the military government. These poor Guatemalans were demanding the right to own and farm land, to send their children to school, and to receive medical care. Maria had paid little attention to the talk.

"They must be crazy," she thought. The poor in Guatemala have never had these things. How did they expect to get them now? Besides, the Mendez family wanted nothing to do with any fighting.

Yet on this morning, September 10, 1980, the hidden war came to San Miguel Acatán. It pounded on the door of the Mendez family. It forced its way into their lives. Like a volcano, the war erupted and spread violence, death, and suffering throughout the village.

Don José

Karin Mendez

 Karin Mendez was not yet born when her family fled Guatemala. Her grandfather, Don José Mendez, left first. Just days after the guerrillas appeared that morning in 1980, Don José escaped San Miguel Acatán with the help of the village priest. He traveled north, through Guatemala, into Mexico, and on to the United States. In Florida, he found a job and an apartment.

Don José urged his family to join him. Three months later Karin's mother, Maria Mendez, her grandmother Guadalupe, her brother Josito, and six aunts and uncles escaped Guatemala. They sought safety and a new life in the United States.

On July 2, 1984, at St. Mary's Hospital in West Palm Beach, Florida, Karin became the first of the Mendez family to be born in the United States. Karin is now 10 years old and a fourth grader at Palm Springs Elementary School in Lake Worth, a city just south of West Palm Beach. She is the only daughter of Maria and Juan José Mendez (Don José's son). Karin has three brothers—José (called "Josito" as a baby), now 14; Juan Carlos, 6; and Jesus, 4.

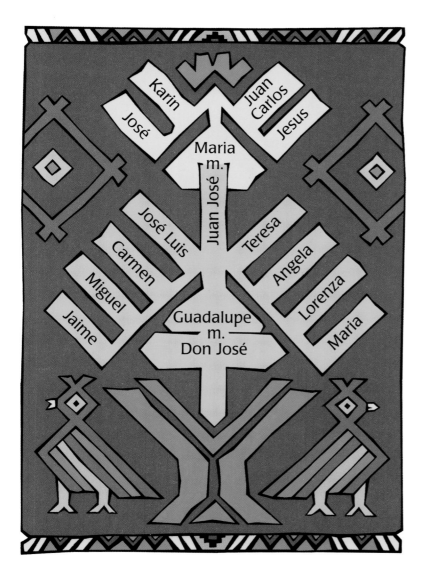

Karin
José
Juan Carlos
Jesus
Maria
m.
Juan José
José Luis
Teresa
Carmen
Angela
Miguel
Lorenza
Jaime
Guadalupe
m.
Don José
Maria

This family tree traces Karin and her brothers to their grandparents, Don José and Guadalupe.

Karin enjoys being in Ms. Rowe's fourth-grade class.

"Music, art, and gym are my favorite classes, but spelling is my best," Karin says, fingering her raven-black hair. She proudly shows her latest report card—all A's and B's. Ms. Susan Rowe, her fourth-grade teacher, says Karin is a model student.

Centuries ago in Guatemala, the Maya Indians founded what some people say was one of the most brilliant civilizations in the Americas. Karin is a descendant of these Mayas, and she resembles them in many ways. Her coal-black eyes are the size and shape of large marbles. Her skin is a cinnamon color. She has thick, straight hair and a long forehead that slopes to a broad nose. When Karin smiles—which is often—her sharp cheekbones draw high, and her face seems especially round.

Soft-spoken and courteous, Karin speaks English clearly, with no trace of an accent. But at home, she uses a form of Spanish that includes many Mayan words. Like the other girls in her class, Karin wears T-shirts, jean skirts, and tennis shoes. Spaghetti with meat sauce is her favorite meal, and *The Secret Garden* her favorite video. Her pets include a turtle named Lola, a lime-green parakeet, and a stray cat.

On weekends, and in the summer when the sun bakes Florida, Karin and her older brother José visit their *tuco,* a Mayan word for grandfather. Don José and Guadalupe's home is a 15-minute bike ride from

Karin's house. Karin and José cool off in the backyard pool, then head inside for a lunch of *tortillas*. These thin pancakes are made of cornmeal or white flour and stuffed with grilled chicken or black beans.

Karin sometimes sits with her favorite cousin, four-year-old Cristina, at the big table in the den. Outside the picture window, banana trees droop in the heat. The two girls admire the photographs of their relatives on the wall. They especially like the wedding picture of Chepe and Guadalupe. What a handsome couple they were!

Don José reads a story to Cristina, Karin's younger cousin (right). *The girls' favorite family picture is a wedding portrait of their grandparents* (above).

Karin has never set foot in Guatemala. She knows about the country of her ancestors only from the stories her parents, grandparents, and other Guatemalans in Lake Worth tell her. When Karin hears these stories, she feels connected to an ancient world, a world that is part of her, part of who she is today.

"Tuco, Tuco, tell us a story," Karin and Cristina beg Don José. Before he goes to work at the Centro Guatemalteco, their grandfather might tell a Mayan folktale, like the one about the Red Witch of the Hill.

Called Ajitz Co'xol, this witch had a red face like a devil. Ajitz Co'xol lived on a hill in Guatemala called

Many Guatemalans in the United States miss the festivals—such as this Easter celebration (left)—that they enjoyed in their homeland. Guatemalan refugees and immigrants can get help adjusting to life in the United States at the Centro Guatemalteco, where Don José (above) works. He answers phones, directs questions, and helps anxious Guatemalans feel at ease.

Ancient Maya—the ancestors of the Guatemalan Indians—wore brightly painted masks at harvest festivals.

Chua Cristilin. She was very mean to the Tzutuhil Indians who lived nearby. The Indians grew tired of being mistreated, so they came up with a plan. They turned into their spirit forms—owls, hawks, eagles, and other animals. Then they captured Ajitz Co'xol and forced her to leave. But when the red-faced witch left, she took all the riches of the hill with her and left the people poor.

Mostly though, the girls want to hear about San Miguel Acatán. They want to know more about this distant land that sometimes feels so close. "Life was so simple there," Don José remembers. "No television, no electricity. There was nothing to do, but we were happy." He describes the sweet smell of cardamom growing in the fields and of coffee beans, freshly harvested. And when Don José pictures the magnificent sunsets behind the Cuchamatanes Mountains, his face has a faraway look.

"Tell us more, Tuco. Tell us more about Guatemala," the girls plead. "Why did our family have to leave?"

The Mendez family made their home near the Cuchamatanes Mountains in western Guatemala.

Roughly the size of Tennessee, Guatemala is a country in Central America. To the north lies Mexico. To the east is Belize. El Salvador and Honduras are Guatemala's neighbors to the south. A farming country, Guatemala grows mainly bananas, corn, cotton, coffee, and sugarcane. Nearly half of Guatemala's 10.6 million people are Indians, descendants of the great Mayas.

Clues to the Mayan past can be found in many parts of Guatemala. Around the year 300 B.C., Maya Indians began building religious temples and burial tombs. The remains of these structures still stand at Tikal and other sites. A ruler presided over one of dozens of large city-states, such as Tikal and Yaxchilan, where 10,000 or more people lived.

Around A.D. 300, the Mayas developed one of their biggest accomplishments—a writing system. With writing, the Mayas could now record all they had learned about mathematics and astronomy. The Indians developed a calendar, too. But the holy men and

rulers kept that to themselves. They used the calendar to interpret the messages of the gods and other supernatural forces, since the Mayas believed these forces ruled the world.

Mayan civilization reached its peak around A.D. 790. Over the next several hundred years, for unknown reasons, Mayas began to move away from the cities and into the countryside.

In the 1500s, Spanish adventurers looking for new trade routes sailed across the Atlantic Ocean and began to explore the Americas. As they went, these *conquistadores* (conquerors) seized land, power, and wealth from the local peoples. In 1524 a Spaniard named Pedro de Alvarado ventured into Guatemala from Mexico. Alvarado and other conquistadores carried strange diseases that killed many of the local Indians.

For many reasons, the light-skinned Spaniards believed they were better than the dark Indians. The conquistadores claimed Guatemala as a colony of faraway Spain and outlawed Indian culture—language, religion, and customs. The idea that light-skinned peo-

Steep steps lead to the altar of a temple at the ruins of Tikal, an ancient Mayan city in northern Guatemala.

Pedro de Alvarado of Spain conquered Guatemala in 1524.

ples are better than dark-skinned peoples lingers to this day and causes problems for many Guatemalans.

In 1821 Guatemala declared its independence from Spain. Since then, the harsh rulers from Spain have been replaced by dictators and military strongmen of Spanish descent who have made Guatemala their home. The 1970s were an especially difficult time. Those who said anything against the government faced arrest. Once in jail, prisoners were tortured or killed, or they were "disappeared," never to be heard from again. Many Guatemalans feared their own government.

The military leaders sometimes stole money that other nations had loaned the government. This money was meant to build schools and buy medicines. Instead military leaders and their business friends got rich, while many of the community projects were never even started.

Guatemala splintered into two classes of people. In one very small group, people lived in mansions, owned huge *haciendas* (farms), and enjoyed every kind

of luxury. About 90 percent of the people, however, were struggling to survive. They labored from sunrise to sunset to earn only meager pay. Young children worked instead of going to school. Doctors were scarce, and children died from diarrhea and other conditions with known cures.

Nothing seemed to change the unfair system. Eventually, frustration among the poor boiled over into armed conflict. Many angry Guatemalans believed that the only way to change the country was to fight the corrupt government. These people formed the Guerrilla Army of the Poor and other similar groups.

The Guatemalan government accused these rebel guerrillas of trying to ruin the country. In 1978 General Fernando Romeo Lucas García ordered his troops to take control of the Guatemalan government. He began using the military to get rid of the guerrillas. The period between 1978 and 1982 marked the bloodiest fighting. Up to 30,000 people may have been killed, most of them Indians.

Years later mass graves were uncovered where the military had executed whole villages, including women and children. Many bodies showed signs of torture. Nowadays, Guatemala is still among the poorest countries in the Americas, and fighting still continues. The Indians—descendants of the once-mighty Mayan nation—are among the poorest of the poor.

While some Guatemalans live in expensive homes (facing page), *most of the population struggles to make a living. In poor villages, women often gather at lakes and streams to wash their families' clothes by hand* (left).

After working in Guatemala's cornfields (left) *as a boy, Don José opened a store, where he sold items such as handmade sweaters and blankets* (facing page). *The whole family, including Guadalupe and the couple's oldest son Miguel* (below), *worked in the shop.*

 Don José was born and raised in San Miguel Acatán. As a young boy and as a teenager, he carried firewood and harvested *milpa*. This type of corn was the staple of the Guatemalan diet, just as it had been for the ancient Mayas. Don José worked from sunrise to sunset. He often missed school to help with the harvest. Then he spent six years digging in underground mines. The job was dangerous, but he earned more money than he could in the fields. For Don José and most poor people in Guatemala, jobs were scarce and education was a luxury.

When he was 23, Don José had a dream that changed his life. "This was like a vision and voice from God. In the dream, I was living in my house when a car pulled up. All kinds of products were loaded onto the shelves in the house. 'Take care of it. It is yours,' a voice told me. But when I looked on the shelves, they were bare. From that dream, the idea for my *bodega* (store) was born."

With sweat and patience, Don José labored to make La Migueleña, the name he gave his bodega, successful. His wife and nine children—Miguel, Juan José, José Luis, Jaime, Carmen, Angela, Maria, Teresa, and Lorenza—helped him. They sold soap, sugar, Coca-Cola, and fine, handmade sweaters. The items were loaded onto mules and delivered to the customers' homes, sometimes far away in the mountains.

For the first time in his life, Don José was earning enough money. He was hardworking and honest. Most people in San Miguel liked Don José, and they even asked him to be mayor. "No," he told them, "I just want to run my business."

"The store made money for many years," Don José recalls. "It wasn't until about 1980 that we realized that some people were jealous. They thought we were like the rich people who exploited the poor."

Don José was appointed to be a military commissioner. His job was to ensure order in San Miguel.

To protect his family, Don José knew he had to leave Guatemala before the guerillas (above) *returned to San Miguel.*

Because some people thought he was wealthy and because he held the position of commissioner, the guerrillas who came to San Miguel believed Don José sided with the military government. To them, he was an enemy. So on the morning of September 10, 1980, the guerrillas pounded on Don José's door.

 Like Maria, Don José also was awoken by the gunfire. His heart pounded as the shots grew closer. Then he heard his name. "Chepe Mendez!" the soldiers yelled. Puh-koo! A gunshot sounded. The portrait of Jesus Christ rattled on the wall above Don José's head.

Maria called to the guerrillas, "What do you want? Do you promise that if my father-in-law comes out you won't harm him?"

"We won't kill him, but tell him to surrender and lay down his weapons," the men shouted back.

Don José had no idea what would happen. He did what he felt best to protect his family. He walked out of the two-story mud-brick house and surrendered. He had no weapon, but the guerrillas believed he did. They grabbed him and twisted his arms behind his back. They marched him to the jail that, as commissioner, *he* was supposed to oversee.

That same morning, another man the guerrillas believed to be a government supporter was killed. Two others were wounded. The guerrillas questioned Don José for several hours, then released him, unharmed.

The guerrillas left San Miguel. They knew the government would send soldiers, lots of soldiers, to hunt the rebels down. But a few days later, the guerrillas sent a scribbled note to Don José. "We'll be back, and next time you may not escape alive."

Don José knew the guerrillas meant what they said. If he ignored their threat and did nothing, he might bring harm to his family. But the guerrillas often blocked the roads out of San Miguel Acatán, so how could he leave?

He telephoned his oldest son, Miguel, who had left Guatemala in 1977. Miguel worked as a mechanic in a factory in Los Angeles, California. "Come to the United States, Papa. Stay with my family and me. I will help you find work," Miguel urged.

Don José visited Father Andrés, the local Catholic priest. Father Andrés knew Don José to be a good, religious man. He saw the danger Don José risked. Together, they came up with a plan. Don José told his family he would be leaving for Miguel's. He planned to return to Guatemala when the danger passed.

The next morning, Father Andrés loaded his jeep with boxes of garbage for the weekly delivery to a

Don José headed to Los Angeles, where Miguel and his family live.

town called Huehuetenango, or "Place of the Ancients." Hidden under the trash, Don José shifted and tried to ignore the stench. With the priest at the wheel, the jeep passed easily through the guerrilla roadblocks. As the jeep bumped along the mountain road toward Huehuetenango, Don José didn't know that he might never return to San Miguel Acatán. He only knew that if he stayed, he risked death for himself and his family.

As the guerrillas had feared, the government army did come to San Miguel. The military bombed the mountains and tried to force the guerrillas to surrender. The army suspected that the poor in San Miguel and other towns were helping the peasant soldiers, so the army tortured and killed many innocent people. The fighting grew bloodier and fiercer.

Guatemala's military government believed nearly everyone in San Miguel was a guerilla. The government soldiers (above) *spent little time separating the guilty from the innocent. Many of both were killed.* (facing page) *This map shows the route that Don José took from Guatemala to his new home in Florida.*

In Huehuetenango, the regional capital, Don José arranged for a tourist visa to cross into Mexico. He continued north, spent the night in Tapachula, on the Mexican border, then headed for the capital of Mexico. In Mexico City, one of the world's largest cities, Don José searched a map for Jardin Balbuena Street. Then he took a taxi to the home of Carlos Bernal Salinas.

Los Angeles, California

Tijuana

UNITED STATES

MEXICO

GULF OF
MEXICO

Miami, Florida

PACIFIC
OCEAN

Caribbean
Sea

Mexico
City

• • • • Jeep
– – – Bus
——— Plane

GUATEMALA

Jeep
route

San Miguel Acatán

Miles
0   200   400
0 200 400
Kilometers

Tapachula
Huehuetenango

To escape the violence in their country, hundreds of thousands of Guatemalan Indians fled to Mexico. For years they survived in dusty tent cities. Some warfare continued in Guatemala in the 1990s, while the guerrillas and the government tried to work out a peace settlement.

"Oh yes, I remember, our sons studied together in Guatemala. Of course I will help you." Mr. Salinas invited Don José to stay.

On the morning of the fourth day, Don José clanked the gate behind him at Mr. Salinas's house. He boarded a bus and traveled 14 hours to Tijuana, a Mexican city on the border between Mexico and the United States.

At the La Playa Hotel in Tijuana, Don José was told to look for a certain *coyote*—a person who sneaks illegal immigrants into a new country. He found the man and paid him $350. Lucky for Don José, this coyote knew his business. He knew how to slip people into the United States at places where the border guards would not catch them. Often, immigrants trying to cross the border are caught and sent back to Mexico. They scrape together enough money to try again and again to reach the United States—the Land of Opportunity.

On September 29, 1980, Don José knocked on his son's door in Los Angeles. Don José spent eight days in this southern California city. But he didn't like it. Los Angeles was filled with smog and with immigrants desperate for any job. In Guatemala, people had talked about Florida, about a place called Indiantown. Guatemalans had gone there to work in the fields. Don José called a friend from San Miguel Acatán who had gone to Florida several years before.

"¿Sí? Don José? Oh, hermano (brother)! How good to hear the voice of another Guatemalan. . . . You want to come to Florida? I will help you if I can. Do you need some money? . . . I can help a little."

Don José borrowed $400 for plane fare and flew to Miami, Florida. His friend met him at the airport and helped him find work with a construction company in Lake Worth. The pay Don José earned on this job was better than if he had gone to Indiantown, where farm work was the only option.

Don José flew to Miami where a friend helped him find a job. "Everything in the United States moves so fast. It's such a change. In our little town in Guatemala you never even saw a car. Here, in this big city, there's television, places to go, always so much to do," notes Don José.

BECOMING U.S. CITIZENS

Indians from Guatemala first arrived in South Florida in 1980. These Mayan refugees had fled political turmoil in their own country and had made their way to Indiantown—a small farming community 25 miles northwest of West Palm Beach. They had not gotten permission from the U.S. government to come to the United States, so they were considered illegal immigrants, or aliens.

At Indiantown, a Catholic priest named Father Frank O'Loughlin had set up a haven for illegal immigrants. At that time, little information was available about the hidden war in Guatemala. Few of the U.S. border patrol agents and immigration officials knew anything about the violence in Guatemala. But Father Frank had

learned of the desperate situation in that country. He also knew that U.S. officials did not recognize the persecution that the Indians faced in Guatemala and would send them back to their country.

Father Frank instructed the refugees in Indiantown not to cooperate with U.S. officials. "We will try to help you in court," he said as he handed out cards with the message *No firmes nada; no digas nada; llama al abogado* (Don't sign anything; don't say anything; call the lawyer). Lawyers from the Florida Rural Legal Services and from the American Friends Service Committee represented Guatemalan Indians who had been put in prison because they did not have legal papers

saying they could
remain in the United States.

Most of the Guatemalans understood no English and only a little Spanish. Instead they spoke one of 22 Mayan dialects—Kanjobal or Mam or Quiché. Father Frank spoke for them, pleading their cases before immigration judges. He told the judges—and anyone else who would listen—about the terrible hidden war. Father Frank insisted that the Guatemalans had rights in the United States. Like other people that have come here to escape suffering, they were protected by U.S. laws, he argued.

Afraid to return to Guatemala, the Mendez family remained illegally in the United States for several years. In 1986 a new immigration law was passed that helped them become legal residents. The Immigration Reform and Control Act (IRCA) gave the Mendez family and other illegal immigrants a chance to become naturalized, or legal, U.S. citizens if they signed up by May 4, 1988.

They needed to show bank statements, receipts for rent paid on an apartment, or other documents to prove that they had been living and working in the United States since January 1, 1982. The Centro Guatemalteco, where Don José now works, helped the Mendez family obtain the papers they needed to remain legally in the United States.

Six and sometimes seven days a week, Don José cut and sawed. For $3.50 an hour, he shimmied up and down a ladder, leaned over the roof and hammered roof trusses. Unused to the hard physical work, his hands grew blistered and sore.

"For so many years I worked in my store. That's what I knew, but now I had to work where I could. At night I sometimes read my Bible and asked myself, 'How can it be that I am going to end my life here in this strange place doing this work?'"

When government soldiers came to San Miguel, it became too dangerous for Guadalupe (above) and her family to stay.

 Soon after Don José arrived in Florida, Guadalupe called. "The guerrillas came again. They threatened us. Last night, a drunk man threw a stone through the window. And the government soldiers have come. At night, we are not allowed to leave our houses. We are afraid. What can we do?"

The danger didn't pass. It grew worse. Don José was worried about his family, and he realized he couldn't follow his plan to return home to San Miguel soon. It was too risky.

"Sell the truck, the store, and other properties," he told his wife on the phone. "Sell whatever you can and come, come to Florida."

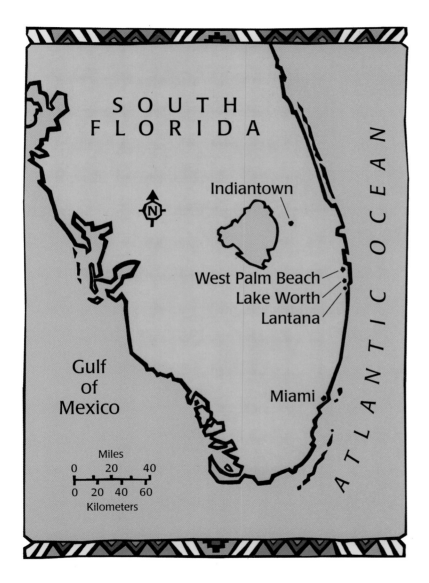

SOUTH FLORIDA

Indiantown

West Palm Beach
Lake Worth
Lantana

Gulf
of
Mexico

Miami

ATLANTIC OCEAN

Miles
0   20   40
0 20 40 60
Kilometers

The Mendez family settled in Lake Worth, Florida. Many Guatemalans settled here because they could find work in the agricultural fields nearby.

"But how can I leave tomorrow? I haven't even said good-bye to my parents. No, I can't go," Maria told her mother-in-law. Maria had lived all her life in San Miguel Acatán, except when she had attended a school for girls in the capital, Guatemala City.

Soon after she returned to San Miguel Acatán, she met Juan José. The two began to date—secretly. Teenage girls like Maria were not allowed to see boys alone. But when Maria turned 18, she and Juan José got married.

Shortly before Don José fled Guatemala, Juan José had left for the southern United States, where he hoped to find a better life. He worked in the fields picking vegetables, following the harvests from state to state. But having her husband already in the United

It was hard for Maria to leave San Miguel, where she had met and married Juan José (above). *She knew she would greatly miss her parents* (left, with Guadalupe and her young daughter Teresa to the far left).

Many Guatemalans come to the United States to work in the fields. Called migrant workers, these laborers travel to wherever the harvest is. Juan José was a migrant worker at the time when Maria and little José left San Miguel.

States did not make it any easier for Maria to leave her homeland. She was only 21.

"No, I don't want to leave San Miguel," Maria told Guadalupe. "How can I leave behind my parents and everything I have known?"

But Maria recognized the dangers the family faced, and she had seen the first of the killings and the horror of the war. "I'll go," she said, then almost refused again when Guadalupe told her she could take nothing. Only the clothes on her back.

When Maria (above) *crossed the U.S.-Mexican border she wondered what her new life would be like. Crossing the border is difficult. Many people are stopped by the U.S. border patrol* (facing page).

 Maria gazed up into a sky filled with stars. She peered into the darkness toward the *frontera*, the invisible border separating Mexico and the United States. She had traveled for days, and her belly ached with hunger. The meals she had cooked at Mr. Salinas's house in Mexico City were only memories now. The bus to Tijuana had been hot and crammed with people. The Mendez family had little money, and none to spare for food. In Tijuana at the coyote's house, she had eaten two tacos. But the spicy sauce on the tacos had upset her stomach, and now, tight like a knot, it grumbled.

Maria waited for the signal from the coyote. Then she felt the surge as the others began to run toward the dried riverbed—the border. Maria drew Josito, now 11 months old, close and ran like never before. They all ran. Guadalupe and José Luis and Jaime and Carmen and Angela and Teresa and Lorenza.

Once across the border, they piled into a pickup truck. "Stay down," the man hissed. Maria ducked under the front seat with little José. She gasped for breath.

"What will our new lives be like in the United States?" Maria wondered. "How will we survive? We don't know the language, the customs." Her mind raced. Maria closed her eyes and tried to doze as the truck rumbled into the darkness.

Maria stayed only one week at Miguel's home in Los Angeles. Then on December 14, 1980, she said good-bye to the rest of the family and flew to Miami with her infant son and her brother-in-law Jaime. Don José met them at the airport, and they drove to the tiny apartment he had rented near downtown West Palm Beach. Guadalupe and Carmen came soon after, and Juan José also joined his family.

In San Miguel Acatán, according to Guatemalan custom, Maria and Juan José had lived with Don José and Guadalupe. Now that they were in Florida, the young couple again lived with Juan José's parents. They had no choice. They knew no one and spoke only a few words of English. Money was scarce. So six adults and little José crammed into a one-bedroom apartment. Maria worried about the neighborhood.

She knew people who had been robbed, and drug addicts and drunkards wandered in the area at night.

As a girl in Guatemala, Maria had learned to sew traditional women's dresses called *huipiles*. But in West Palm Beach, no one wanted the brightly colored huipiles. Maria was hired to sew men's shirts in a factory. For this tedious work, she earned only $3 an hour. Juan José labored on a construction crew during the day, and at night he cooked in a Mexican restaurant.

Maria is teaching Karin how to sew huipiles—traditional Guatemalan dresses.

Karin and Maria (above) *share a joke. Karin's younger brothers—Carlos and Jesus—shoot baskets* (facing page) *in the family's driveway.*

After a year in the cramped living quarters, Maria, Juan José, and little José moved to an apartment in Lantana, a smaller city farther south. This apartment had an air conditioner, but they didn't use it. Neither Maria nor Juan José knew how. They hadn't even had electricity in San Miguel Acatán, let alone air-conditioning.

Over the next dozen years, the family moved from one apartment to the next, from one problem to another. At one house, the stench from a leaky septic tank soured the air. Another house was infested with roaches that nibbled holes in the childrens' clothes.

By March 1994, Maria and Juan José had managed to save enough money to buy a house. The Mendez home in Lake Worth is a single-story white cement house just blocks from a bustling four-lane roadway. The street is lined with typical American restaurants and stores—Checkers Hamburgers, Tire Kingdom, Barnett Bank, and J&M Beer Depot. Karin's favorite restaurant, Sizzler, is just down the street.

In the grassy front yard, banana trees with big leafy fronds wave in the warm Florida breeze. A small garden of vegetables and wild herbs grows next to the carport. Carlos and Jesus dribble a basketball on the cement driveway. A shiny red Toyota pickup truck and a pale-blue Corsica are parked under a tree. Around back, the garage has been converted into Maria's sewing room and an extra kitchen.

 The sky is still dark when the back screen door squeaks, and Maria Mendez approaches the stone steps leading to the garage. She is the first one up on Saturdays. Juan José wakes soon after, eats breakfast, then heads to work. Karin—"I'm such a sleepyhead"—and José get up later. The family works side by side to prepare stacks of tortillas and *tamales*—cornmeal mixed with chunks of meat and wrapped in banana leaves or corn husks for flavor. They dice fresh red tomatoes, then add chopped herbs and spicy peppers to make a hot sauce called salsa.

Every Saturday, Maria and the children prepare more than 100 tamales. They load their bright red pickup truck with pans of tamales and other traditional foods for delivery to Guatemalans in the community. Maria's cooking earns extra money for the family. And her customers are happy for the tamales—a food that they can't buy anywhere else in Lake Worth and that takes hours to prepare. Maria dreams that one day she'll open a restaurant.

Maria makes piles of tortillas (left) *and chops hot peppers* (above) *to mix into her salsa. She doesn't need any cookbooks. She knows the recipes by heart.*

Jesus enjoys an after-school snack of beans and tortillas with cheese.

This Saturday is special. Maria has agreed to take food to a nearby park, where the Guatemalan boys' soccer team is playing. It's still early in the day, but the Florida sun is already hot. Maria decides to prepare *horchata*, a sweet drink made from almonds and flavored with cinnamon.

During the game, the parents of the other team cheer and yell, but the Guatemalans stand quietly on the sidelines. They nod and smile, but clap only for an exceptional play. Guatemalans do not show much emotion. They are a quiet people. Years of violence in

Boys from the Guatemalan soccer team cheer on their teammates (left), *while Maria and other women prepare a post-game feast* (below).

Guatemala have made them suspicious. To talk to the "wrong" person might get them arrested. This could mean death. At the park, the Guatemalans talk softly among themselves, sharing stories about a better job or a new baby.

When the game is over, the Guatemalans gather to enjoy the foods Maria and the other women have made. They sip iced horchata and munch tortillas. For the Guatemalans, who work hard every day in a strange, fast-paced culture, the soccer game provides a rare relaxing afternoon among friends.

After school on Friday, Jesus and Juan Carlos sprawl on the living room carpet. Their eyes are glued to the big TV in the corner, where Spiderman's webbed body slinks across the screen. Turned up loud, the television fills the room, but Karin doesn't notice. She's just arrived home from school and already has arranged her books and papers on the dining room desk where she studies.

"I study until I finish my homework," the 10-year-old says matter-of-factly, as if youngsters everywhere finished their weekend homework on Friday afternoon.

Karin always does her homework (above) *right after school—even on Fridays. Jesus likes to watch TV and spend time with his mom* (right) *before dinner.*

Karin loves school this year. "Ms. Rowe is my favorite teacher yet," she says. The Palm Springs Elementary teacher, lively and friendly, returns the compliment. "Karin is a model student—studious, friendly, and generous."

Karin gets along with just about everyone, but her best friends—Melissa, Cindy, Dawn, and Jennifer—are also children of immigrant parents. About half of Karin's classmates are from families whose parents

Carlos watches his sister work on a computer at school (left). *Karin studies hard to earn good grades, such as this A+ in spelling* (above).

Karin has many friends at school. But some kids tease her because her parents come from another country.

have come from other countries. The girls tell secrets, giggle, and whisper in English. It's the language they use with their friends, though they also understand the native languages of their parents.

Karin's brother José, now 14, attends John I. Leonard High School. Unlike Karin's class, José's class has only two immigrant children. Like most teenagers, José doesn't want to feel different. He wants to fit in and be treated like "one of the guys."

After she finishes her homework, Karin likes to read (left). Saturday Market—*her favorite book—describes goods such as beans, corn, and seeds* (below), *which are sold in Guatemalan markets.*

Karin doesn't really care to watch TV. She prefers to draw—especially bears and flowers—or to read. At school, she reads only English. At home, though, her favorite book is one in English and Spanish.

"In *Saturday Market* they bring all the stuff to the market to sell. I like the pictures and enjoy pronouncing the words, like '*tortilla*,' or '*sandalias*' (sandals)."

The story is familiar to Karin's mom. In San Miguel Acatán, Maria often shopped at an outdoor market like the one in the book. Maria wants Karin to know about Guatemala. She wants Guatemalan traditions and culture to be a part of the lives of all her children. Although she is thankful her children live in the United States, Maria also wants them to know where they come from.

Maria remembers the street markets where she shopped as a girl and is glad that Karin is learning about life in Guatemala.

Teaching her children about the traditions and customs of Guatemala is important to Maria.

"There are so many memories, so many customs, so many beautiful things to remember about Guatemala," Maria says. "The Mayan stories my grandfather used to tell are especially important. They have so much wisdom."

In the Mendez home, Guatemalan tradition is kept alive in part through food. Guatemalan foods are served regularly. Karin's father prefers Maria's homemade tortillas and tamales to fast food. Juan José enjoys crispy *tostadas* (deep-fried corn chips) and fresh salsa—his wife's specialties.

Karin often starts her day with a breakfast of tortillas with black beans or scrambled eggs. On cooler days, she eats *mox,* a cereal like oatmeal sweetened with sugar, cinnamon, and milk. Karin gets a coupon for free lunch at school, so she eats at the cafeteria. Like many students, she prefers the food served in her home.

For dinner, Karin and her brothers set the table. They pour water and serve the food. Dinner is an important part of the day, and the Mendez family eats together.

For dinner, Karin makes tortillas (left), *which will be stuffed with shredded beef* (above).

On the bookshelf near the dinner table stands a statue of San Miguel, or Saint Michael, the patron saint of the family's village in Guatemala. Saint Michael blesses the harvests and brings good fortune to San Miguel Acatán. In the Mendez home in Lake Worth, the statue watches over the family meal. After dinner, the Mendez children sit and listen to the stories their mother and father sometimes tell about their country.

A statue of Saint Michael (above), *the patron saint of San Miguel Acatán, watches over the Mendez family as they eat their meal* (right).

After dinner, Karin likes to play with Jesus in the backyard, while Carlos pokes Lola, a pet turtle.

For one week in September every year, Guatemalans in San Miguel Acatán celebrate the Festival de San Miguel. Farmers come from the mountains, from the surrounding villages, sometimes from as far away as Huehuetenango to honor Saint Michael.

Soon after coming to Florida, Don José organized the first San Miguel Day celebration in Lake Worth. Don José wanted to help Guatemalans remember the country they had left behind, and he wanted to help them honor their rich culture and past. Each year the festival has grown. Today it's the most awaited day of the year for the 10,000 or so Guatemalans who live in the area.

On this Saturday night in September, the auditorium at Sacred Heart Church brims with excitement. Father Frank O'Loughlin, the Catholic priest who has helped Guatemalans in Florida, crowns the princess of this year's festival.

At the Festival de San Miguel, three musicians tap playful tunes on the marimba, a xylophone-like instrument.

Father Frank crowns the festival princess.

The crowd sings the Guatemalan national anthem. Then the Mayan culture is honored with readings. Dr. Jaime Zapata, the energetic director of the Centro Guatemalteco where Don José works, stands at the microphone. Don Jaime invites Don José and others who have organized the festival to come on stage.

Dressed all in white, Don José looks young and handsome, like in his wedding picture. Guadalupe has pressed every wrinkle from his pants. His *guayabera*, a long shirt, outlines a trim 58-year-old body.

Karin claps with the crowd. Wearing a colorful huipil sewn by Maria, Karin looks radiant. When Don José is called on stage, Karin beams. She is so proud of her tuco, her grandfather who has done so much for the Guatemalans here. She knows how it has broken his heart to leave Guatemala and all that he had known there.

A theater skit is announced, and Maria Mendez struts on stage with Karin's youngest brother, Jesus, and another friend. Karin laughs at her mother dressed in a man's suit, a pillow stuffed in her belly, and sporting a wide mustache. Everyone enjoys the fun.

The skit is over, and Karin applauds. She is so proud of her mother, her family, and her community. She feels safe here. And happy. She loves her life in the United States, and tonight she is especially proud to be Guatemalan.

Jesus shows off his traditional outfit (left) to other festival-goers. Maria (above) draws laughs from the crowd when she performs a funny skit dressed as a man.

SPANISH PRONUNCIATION GUIDE

bodega (boh-DAY-gah)
cállate querido (KAH-yah-tay kay-REE-doh)
Centro Guatemalteco (SEHN-troh gwah-teh-mahl-TAY-koh)
Chepe (CHEH-pay)
Cuchamatanes (koo-chah-mah-TAH-nays)
Don José Mendez (dohn hoh-SAY MEHN-dehz)
Guadalupe (gwah-dah-LOO-pay)
guayabera (gwah-yah-BEH-rah)
guerrillas (geh-REE-yahs)
horchata (or-CHAH-tah)
huipiles (wee-PEE-lays)
Jaime (HEYE-may)
Jesus (HAY-soos)
Josito (hoh-SEE-toh)
Juan (wahn)
milpa (MEEL-pah)
San Miguel Acatán (sahn mee-GEHL ah-kah-TAHN)
Tapachula (tah-pah-CHOO-lah)
Tijuana (tee-WAH-nah)

MAYAN PRONUNCIATION GUIDE

Ajitz Co'xol (ah-jeetz koh-SHUHL)
Huehuetenango (way-way-TEH-nahn-goh)
Kanjobal (kahn-joh-BAHL)
Mam (mahm)
Maya (MAH-yah)
mox (mohsh)
Quiché (kee-CHAY)
tuco (TOO-koh)

FURTHER READING

Ashabranner, Brent and Paul Conklin. *Children of the Maya: A Guatemalan Indian Odyssey*. New York: Dodd, Mead & Company, 1986.

Castaneda, Omar S. *Abuela's Weave*. New York: Lee & Low Books, 1993.

Cheney, Glenn Alan. *Revolution in Central America*. New York: Franklin Watts, an Impact Book, 1984.

Guatemala in Pictures. Minneapolis: Lerner Publications Company, Geography Department, 1987.

Jacobsen, Peter Otto and Preben Sejer Kristensen. *A Family in Central America*. New York: The Bookwright Press, 1986.

Jenness, Aylette and Lisa W. Kroeber. *A Life of Their Own: An Indian Family in Latin America*. New York: Thomas Y. Crowell & Co., 1975.

Lantier-Sampon, Patricia. *Guatemala is My Home*. Milwaukee: Gareth Stevens Publications, 1993.

Montejo, Victor. *The Bird Who Cleans the World and Other Mayan Fables*. Translated by Wallace Kaufman. Willimantic, CT: Curbstone Press, 1991.

Volkmer, Jane Anne. *Song of the Chirimia, A Guatemalan Folktale*. Minneapolis: Carolrhoda Books, 1990.

ABOUT THE AUTHOR

Michael Malone is a writer and journalist living in Miami. He writes both in Spanish and English on culture and ethnic topics, especially on Latinos in the United States. His articles have appeared in *The New York Times*, *The Washington Post*, *The Miami Herald*, and EFE, the international news wire agency of Spain. He has interpreted, translated, and researched for *Frontline* television documentaries and for several books on Latin America.

PHOTO ACKNOWLEDGMENTS

Cover photographs by Buddy Mays/Travel Stock (left) and Michael Malone (right). All inside photos by Michael Malone except the following: Buddy Mays/Travel Stock, pp. 6, 10, 19, 26 (top), 33; Suzanne Murphy-Larronde, pp. 7, 8, 25; UPI/Bettmann, pp. 9 (top), 12, 28, 30, 39, 41; Inter-American Development Bank, p. 9 (bottom); Laura Westlund, pp. 15, 20, 31, 37; Richard Hunt, pp. 18 (bottom), 24, 27, 46 (top); Kenneth C. Poertner, p. 22; Library of Congress, p. 23; © James Blank, p. 29; UNHCR/H. J. Davies, p. 32; Dr. Roma Hoff, p. 53; Textile cut-ins by Nancy Smedstad